INSIDE A
ROCKET

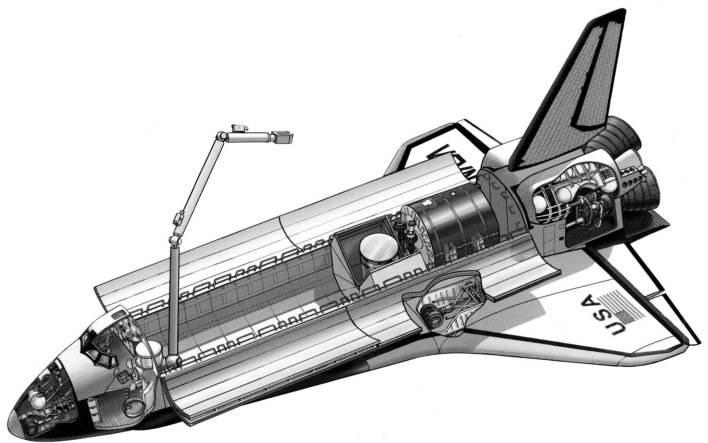

TOM JACKSON

angus

This edition published in 2004
by Angus Books Ltd
12 Ravensbury Terrace
London SW18 4RL

ISBN 1-904594-54-9

FOR BROWN PARTWORKS
Project editor: Tom Jackson
Consultant: Dr. Donald R. Franceschetti
Designer: Sarah Williams
Illustrators: Roger Wade-Walker (main artwork), Mark Walker
Managing editor: Anne O'Daly
Picture researcher: Sean Hannaway

Production by Omnipress,
Eastbourne, UK
Printed and bound in Dubai

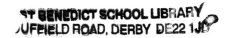

Contents

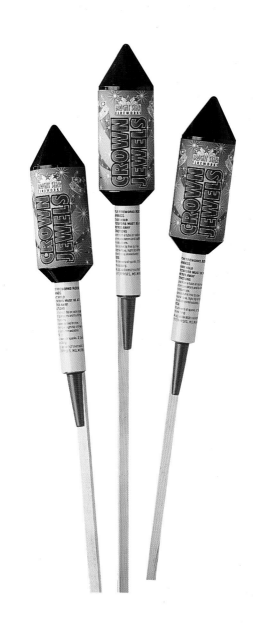

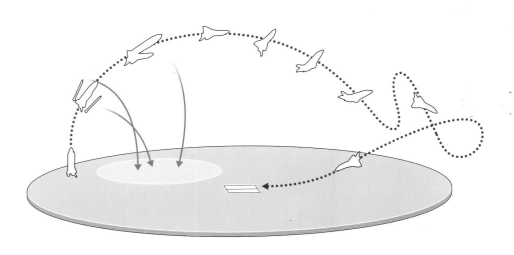

Fig.2.

Rocket into the history books

Simple metal rockets that had gunpowder for fuel were used by soldiers about 200 years ago. This illustration shows how these simple weapons were fired at an enemy.

People have been making rockets for many hundreds of years for many purposes—as fireworks, weapons and vehicles for going into space.

Modern space rockets are just very large, complicated and expensive fireworks. They work in the same way. About 1,000 years ago the first rocket fuel was invented in China. The fuel was called gunpowder and was a mixture of chemicals that burned very hot and fast.

Causing a bang
Gunpowder was first used as an explosive for making loud bangs and bright flashes. About 800 years ago it was used to make firework rockets like the ones used today.

Until the beginning of the 20th century large fireworks were used as weapons. They were fired at enemy soldiers and ships. The line about "the rocket's red glare" in the U.S. national anthem refers to rockets being used in a battle 200 years ago.

Looking to the sky
Nearly 350 years ago a French science-fiction writer had the idea of using rockets to get into space and travel to the Moon. In the 1920s an American scientist named Robert Goddard (1882–1945) made a new type of rocket that would eventually be used to do just that. Instead of using solid fuel like gunpowder, Goddard's rocket used liquid fuels that let the rockets travel faster and farther than ever before.

During World War II (1939–1945) German scientists made flying bombs powered by rockets. People were terrified of these bombs, called V2s, because they travelled faster than sound, and their victims could not hear them coming.

Scientist Robert Goddard in 1925 standing next to one of his early liquid-fuelled rockets.

FACT FILE

○ Russian scientist Konstantin Tsiolkovsky (1857–1935) was the first person to think about the problems of flying into space. He wrote a book about how to navigate in space and return safely to Earth.

○ In 1958 the U.S. government set up the National Aeronautics and Space Administration (NASA) to develop spacecraft and other types of flying machine. NASA is the biggest space organization in the world.

Up, up, and away

After the war the scientists who built the V2 rockets went to the United States and Russia (then called the Soviet Union) and built rockets to carry nuclear bombs to distant targets. In 1957 the Russians launched *Sputnik 1*, the first artificial satellite, using one of these rockets. That started a long competition between Russia and the United States. It was called the space race.

U.S. scientists sent their own rocket into space soon after *Sputnik* was launched, but not before a Russian dog, called Laika, became the first animal to travel into space.

Men in space

In 1961 the Russians again beat the United States by using a rocket to launch the first human, Yuri Gagarin (1934–1968), into orbit. However, over the next eight years the United States built the world's largest rocket and flew people to the Moon.

Rocket engines are still used to take things into space. For example, the space shuttle uses several different rockets. It carries scientists and satellites into space and transports astronauts to and from space stations.

A thousand years after they were invented, rockets took people to the Moon.

Inside a space shuttle

The space shuttles are the most advanced spacecrafts in use today. They are launched using both solid- and liquid-fuelled rocket engines. Unlike any other spacecraft, the shuttles fly back to the Earth like an aeroplane.

FACT FILE

⭕ The first space shuttle was called *Columbia*. It was first launched in 1981. It is still the biggest of the space shuttles.

⭕ Five space shuttles were built: *Challenger*, *Discovery*, *Endeavour* and *Atlantis*, as well as *Columbia*. *Challenger* exploded in 1986.

⭕ Computers on board each space shuttle are used to control the spacecraft's re-entry into the atmosphere and land it safely.

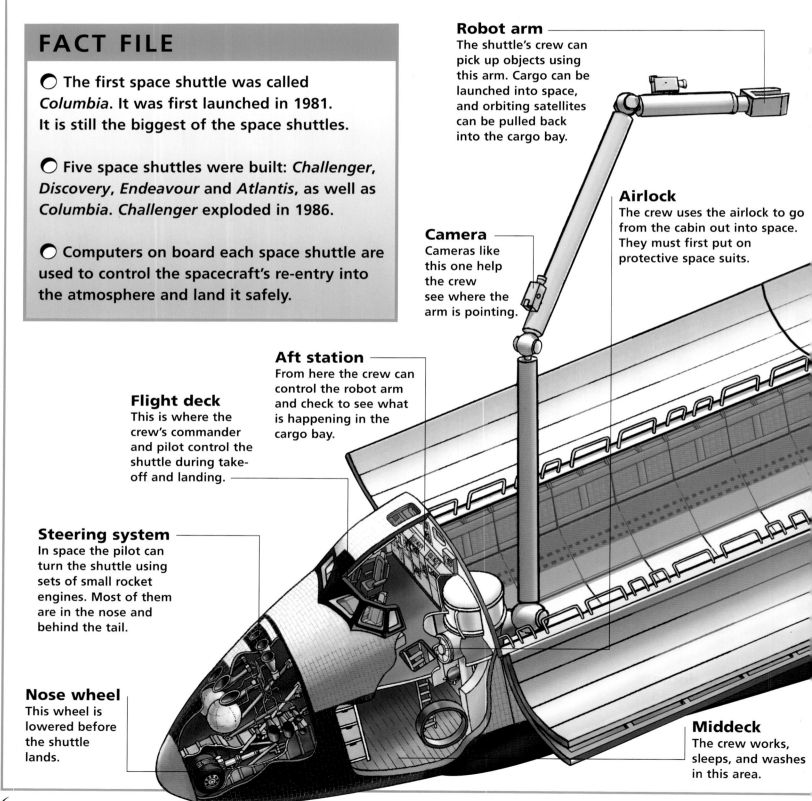

Robot arm
The shuttle's crew can pick up objects using this arm. Cargo can be launched into space, and orbiting satellites can be pulled back into the cargo bay.

Airlock
The crew uses the airlock to go from the cabin out into space. They must first put on protective space suits.

Camera
Cameras like this one help the crew see where the arm is pointing.

Aft station
From here the crew can control the robot arm and check to see what is happening in the cargo bay.

Flight deck
This is where the crew's commander and pilot control the shuttle during take-off and landing.

Steering system
In space the pilot can turn the shuttle using sets of small rocket engines. Most of them are in the nose and behind the tail.

Nose wheel
This wheel is lowered before the shuttle lands.

Middeck
The crew works, sleeps, and washes in this area.

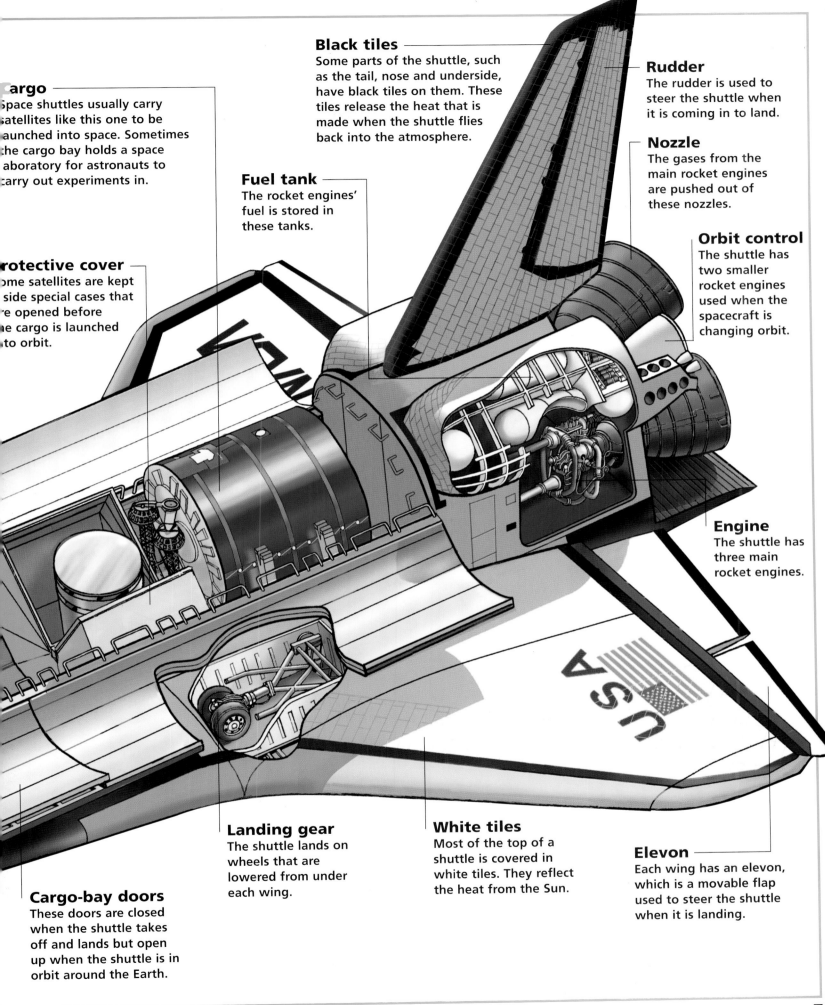

Black tiles
Some parts of the shuttle, such as the tail, nose and underside, have black tiles on them. These tiles release the heat that is made when the shuttle flies back into the atmosphere.

Rudder
The rudder is used to steer the shuttle when it is coming in to land.

Nozzle
The gases from the main rocket engines are pushed out of these nozzles.

Cargo
Space shuttles usually carry satellites like this one to be launched into space. Sometimes the cargo bay holds a space laboratory for astronauts to carry out experiments in.

Fuel tank
The rocket engines' fuel is stored in these tanks.

Orbit control
The shuttle has two smaller rocket engines used when the spacecraft is changing orbit.

Protective cover
Some satellites are kept inside special cases that are opened before the cargo is launched into orbit.

Engine
The shuttle has three main rocket engines.

Landing gear
The shuttle lands on wheels that are lowered from under each wing.

White tiles
Most of the top of a shuttle is covered in white tiles. They reflect the heat from the Sun.

Elevon
Each wing has an elevon, which is a movable flap used to steer the shuttle when it is landing.

Cargo-bay doors
These doors are closed when the shuttle takes off and lands but open up when the shuttle is in orbit around the Earth.

Solid-fuelled rockets

The simplest rockets have solid fuel. When the fuel is set on fire, its exhaust escapes out the nozzle and forces the rocket forward.

Simple rockets, such as fireworks, emergency flares, and even the space shuttle's two launch boosters, have solid fuel inside them. The first rocket fuel was a solid—a mixture of powdered chemicals. When this powder is burned, it makes a mixture of very hot gases. All solid-fuelled rockets work in the same way.

Escaping gas

The hot gases are forced out of the rocket through a small hole called a nozzle. The man who first explained how a rocket works was Sir Isaac Newton (1642–1727), the famous English scientist.

Model rockets like this one use solid fuels. They can fly to thousands of feet.

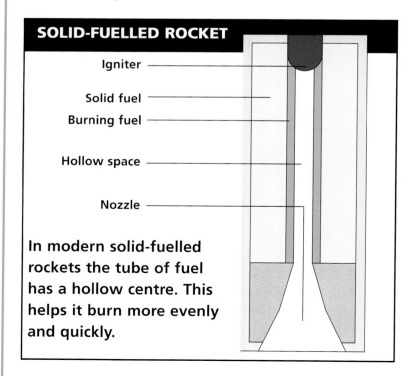

SOLID-FUELLED ROCKET

Igniter

Solid fuel

Burning fuel

Hollow space

Nozzle

In modern solid-fuelled rockets the tube of fuel has a hollow centre. This helps it burn more evenly and quickly.

Newton said that every force causes another force to act in the opposite direction. So, as the exhaust gas is pushed out of the rocket, the rocket is pushed forward by the gas. Because the rocket and exhaust push against each other, rockets can work anywhere—even in the emptiness of space. Other engines, such as propellers, need air to push against.

The first rockets used solid fuel. They were made of a tube of cardboard, paper or cloth attached to a long stick, which helped the

A Taurus rocket lifts off. The rocket uses solid fuel to power it into space.

rocket fly in a straight line. The tube was filled with gunpowder. The bottom of the tube was ignited (set on fire), usually by burning a piece of string (a fuse) attached to the rocket. The fuel began to burn and produce hot gas. The gas flying out of the back of the tube pushed the rocket into the air.

More modern rockets have hard metal cases. They make sure all the exhaust gas leaves the rocket out the back of the tube. A nozzle was added to the rear of the rocket to direct the gas and make the rocket go even faster.

Rockets today

Today solid rocket fuels are very powerful and burn much hotter than gunpowder. The chemical mixture is bound together by special substances called resins to make them safe until they are ignited. Instead of fuses, modern rockets have electric igniters.

FORCES

Ask an adult to help you with this one.

1 Find an open space. The surface should be level and hard. Find a heavy weight, such as a rock or piece of metal.

2 Stand sideways on a still skateboard. Throw the weight to your left. Be careful not to hurt yourself or others nearby.

3 The skateboard and you will move to the right. That is because the force used to throw the rock has created an opposite force that is pushing the skateboard in the other direction.

Liquid-fuelled rockets

Big rockets that can carry people and satellites into space use liquid fuels. Liquid fuels are more powerful than solid ones, and they can make rockets travel faster and farther.

Rockets are used to get into space because they still work outside the Earth's atmosphere, unlike aeroplane engines. Liquid-fuelled rockets are much more powerful than solid-fuelled ones, so they are used for space flights. Unlike solid rockets, liquid-fuelled rockets can be easily turned on and off to help steer craft in space.

Cold gas

Liquid fuels are really gases that have been cooled down to very cold temperatures. That is because it is easier to store liquid than it is to keep gas. Each rocket fuel is made up of two liquids. One is the propellant; the other is the oxidizer. When the propellant and the oxidizer are mixed together and ignited, they react with each other and make lots of heat and exhaust gases.

Like other rockets, the hot exhaust gas is pushed out of the rocket's nozzle and forces the rocket forward. However, the gases produced by burning liquid fuels are much hotter and move out of the nozzle faster than the exhaust from solid-fuelled rockets.

Most liquid-fuelled rocket use liquid oxygen as the oxidizer. Propellants used include petrol and more complex chemicals. The space shuttle's engines use liquid hydrogen as a propellant. The liquid hydrogen combines with the liquid oxygen to make very hot steam.

A liquid-fuelled engine is tested before being attached to the rest of the rocket. This is a Vulcain engine used to power the European Space Agency's Ariane 5 rocket.

LIQUID-FUELLED ROCKET

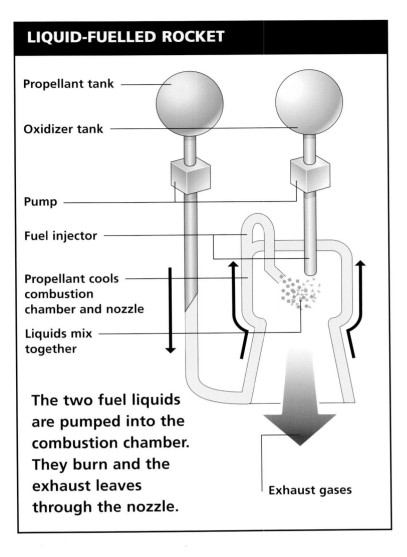

Propellant tank

Oxidizer tank

Pump

Fuel injector

Propellant cools combustion chamber and nozzle

Liquids mix together

Exhaust gases

The two fuel liquids are pumped into the combustion chamber. They burn and the exhaust leaves through the nozzle.

In the chamber

The two liquids are stored in tanks, then pumped into an open space called a combustion chamber, where they mix together. Some fuels react by themselves; others need igniting with a sparkplug, a bit like the one in a car engine. The combustion chamber gets very hot, so the cold liquid fuel is pumped around it and the nozzle to keep them cool and keep them from melting.

The hot gases leave the rocket through the nozzle, which usually has a curved cone shape. The nozzle stops the gas from spreading out once it leaves the rocket; and because the gas is kept together, it makes more force (called thrust). The thrust of a liquid-fuelled rocket can be controlled by pumping more or less fuel into the combustion chamber. More fuel makes more

thrust, and the rocket travels forward faster. Unlike solid-fuelled rockets, liquid-fuelled rockets can be turned off again once they have started burning. This makes liquid-fuelled rockets easier to control. Satellites and the space shuttles use small liquid-fuelled rockets to alter their position in space.

MAKE A ROCKET

You will need a washing-up liquid bottle, two straws (one wider than the other), some modelling clay, tape and some cardboard.

1 Attach the thinner straw to the nozzle on the bottle. Seal it with clay.

2 Cut out cardboard triangles and tape them to the end of the wider straw. Put a cone of clay on the other end.

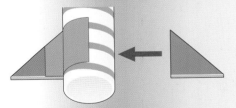

3 Slide the wider "rocket" straw over the thinner "launcher" straw. Launch the rocket by squeezing the bottle very firmly. Point the rocket away from other people.

Saturn V

The Saturn V rockets were built by NASA to take people to the Moon. They are still the largest spacecraft ever built. They were 363 ft (111m) high and carried over 3,000 tons (2,940 tonnes) of fuel.

The Apollo space programme took people to the Moon, and the rocket that was used to do this was the Saturn V. The Saturn V had to be bigger than any rocket used, before or since, because it had to carry so much weight—a crew of three and their equipment—on the 240,000-mile (384,000-km) journey.

Rather than build one huge rocket, scientists at NASA (National Aeronautics and Space Administration) built three smaller rockets on top of each other. There were several reasons for this. The main one was that rocket engines run out of fuel very quickly. So when the first rocket, or stage, as they were called, used up its fuel, it could be jettisoned (thrown away) and the next stage

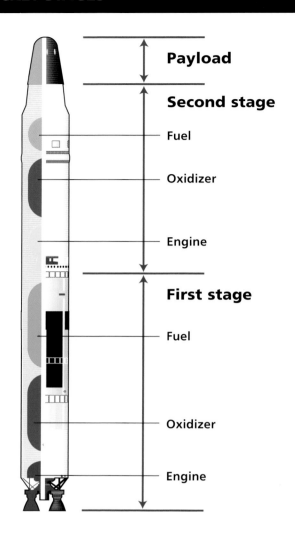

ROCKET STAGES

Payload

Second stage

Fuel

Oxidizer

Engine

First stage

Fuel

Oxidizer

Engine

Large space rockets have sections or stages so they can lift heavy payloads into space. The payload can be satellites or astronauts.

FACT FILE

○ **Other countries use their own types of multistage rockets. Scientists working for the Russian space programme developed the huge Energia rocket. The European Space Agency (ESA) uses Ariane 5.**

○ **The Russian space shuttle *Buran* does not have its own engines and it must be launched using an Energia rocket. After it has reached orbit around the Earth, it glides back to the ground just like the NASA shuttles.**

took over. Because the first stage had been jettisoned, the second stage had less weight to push on the next part of the journey.

The first Saturn V rocket was launched in 1967. The rocket was used six times to take astronauts to the Moon, and it was later adapted to be used to launch Skylab (NASA's only space station). In fact, the main part of Skylab was a specially built third stage of a Saturn V rocket. Instead of holding fuel and a rocket engine, this stage was used as Skylab's orbiting laboratory, living quarters and storage area.

Escape system

This spike contained a small rocket engine that could pull the command module to safety if the rocket failed during launch.

Command module

This tiny cone-shaped module was where the crew sat during launch. It was the only part of the rocket designed to return to Earth with the astronauts. It had a thick heat shield to keep it from burning up as it hit Earth's atmosphere.

Service module

This part of the rocket carried the life-support equipment, such as the air and water. It also had a small rocket engine that the crew used to power their return journey from the Moon.

Lunar module

The lunar module that was to land on the Moon was stored inside this part of the rocket.

Second stage

The second stage's engine had five nozzles. It used liquid hydrogen and oxygen as fuel, and pushed the rocket into orbit around the Earth at more than 14,000 mph (22,400km/h).

First stage

This was the largest of the rocket's stages. It had eight nozzles and used kerosene (aeroplane fuel) and liquid oxygen. The power from this stage pushed the rocket to a speed of 5,400 mph (8,640km/h).

This Saturn V rocket took astronauts and a lunar rover to the Moon in 1971.

White Room

The astronauts were made ready to get into the rocket in the White Room. Attendants then strapped them in before closing the command module hatch.

Tower

The rocket was held upright by the tower until a few seconds before the launch.

Third stage

This final stage only had one nozzle. It also used hydrogen and oxygen as fuel. It was used to power the rocket towards the Moon at 24,300 mph (38,880km/h).

Explosive bolts

The stages were joined together by explosive bolts. When a stage needed to be released, the bolts exploded to detach it from the rest of the rocket.

Fuel and coolant lines

Fuel was pumped into the rocket from the tower. The fuel was also kept very cold by coolants supplied in the same way.

Launch platform

Each Saturn V rocket was assembled on a launch platform. The rocket, platform and tower were then carried to the launchpad.

NASA engineers watch the launch of a space shuttle at the Kennedy Space Center.

At the launchpad

Rockets are dangerous and must be launched from remote places. The launchpad is designed to keep the rocket from blowing itself up.

Space rockets are tall and not very stable, but they must be launched standing up. Rocket launch sites have very large buildings and machines designed to make sure the rocket flies. They are also far from towns and cities in case there is an accident.

The Kennedy Space Center in Florida is the main launch site of NASA, which is in charge of all space flights from the United States.

The space center has a very large building where rockets are put together. The Saturn V rockets that went to the Moon were built inside a single large room, which has one of the highest ceilings in the world. Like those rockets, NASA's space shuttles are also equipped in this building.

On the move

Once the rocket has been put together, it is rolled very slowly to the launchpad on a huge vehicle called a crawler-transporter. The crawler-transporters are designed to carry upright spacecraft. Engineers from the Russian space agency, which launches its rockets from a base in Kazakhstan, Central Asia, build rockets lying down, transport them along railroad tracks and lift them upright onto the launchpad.

A tracked crawler-transporter carries the space shuttle *Endeavour* to the launchpad.

MOBILE LAUNCHERS

This rocket will be towed out to sea and launched from the equator.

Most launch sites are positioned near the equator, the imaginary line that circles the middle of the Earth halfway between the north and south poles. This is because the surface of the Earth is spinning fastest in this area. (At the poles the Earth does not spin at all.) Rockets are launched near the equator to make use of this extra speed and get into space more easily. Some small rockets are launched directly at the equator from a huge floating launchpad. The launchpad is similar to a large oil platform and is towed to the equator in the middle of the Pacific Ocean.

On the pad

Once at the pad the rocket is held in place by a tall tower. The tower allows the astronauts to get into the top of the rocket. It also holds the fuels and coolant pipes in place right up to the moment of launch.

Rocket engines throw out lots of hot flames and gas. Launchpads have concrete gulleys and tunnels that carry these flames away from the rocket. If they were not there, the rocket would set itself on fire and explode when it turned its engine on.

A Saturn V rocket lifts off carrying part of NASA's Skylab space station.

Blast off!

Launching space rockets is a very complicated operation. Hundreds of people are needed to get the rocket into space, then guide it to exactly the right orbit and perform the tasks it was launched for.

Space rockets have to be launched at exactly the right time to make sure they reach their destination. The launch of the rocket is managed by Launch Control in a building near the launchpad. To make sure everything happens at the right time, Launch Control count down the time remaining before the launch.

Forty hours to go

The countdown begins 40 hours before launch. During this time the rocket or shuttle is fuelled and made ready for launch. Everything that is not needed is removed from the pad 24 hours before the launch. Nine minutes before lift-off the launch team reports to the launch director, signalling that everything is ready. The final ten seconds of the launch are counted down over loudspeakers. The engines are started a few seconds before the rocket launches.

FACT FILE

⭘ Most rocket or shuttle launches are broadcast on TV as they happen. They can take place any time of the day or night.

⭘ The space shuttle *Challenger* exploded a few seconds after lift off. This explosion killed all seven members of the crew.

FLYING TO THE MOON

4. Third stage turned off as rocket circles Earth

7. Module heads for the Moon

1. Lift-off using first stage

6. Astronauts' module separates from the empty third stage

2. Second stage fires

5. Third stage fires again, taking the rocket to the Moon

3. Third stage takes over

The different stages of the Moon rockets were used for different parts of the journey.

Once the rocket or shuttle has flown above the tower on the launchpad, the people at Mission Control take over. Mission Control makes sure the rocket or shuttle gets into space and performs the mission it has been launched to do. Information about engines, crew and the position of the rocket is sent by radio to Mission Control. The space shuttles can be controlled almost completely by the people on the ground at Mission Control.

Different stages

Large spacecraft often need to use more than one rocket engine to carry their heavy cargo into space. The space shuttle uses two booster rockets during launch. The Saturn V rockets that took people to the Moon was made of three stages. When one stage ran out of fuel, it was released from the rocket and the next stage was ignited.

Not lost in space

Some rockets launch people and objects to the Moon and other planets, but most end up in orbit around the Earth. When they get into space, rockets are watched closely from the ground.

Rockets are used to take things into space because they carry their own oxidizer and do not need air to burn their fuel. Jet engines would stop working as they left the atmosphere. Once the rocket is in orbit around the Earth, its cargo and crew feel as if they are weightless. However, this is not because gravity has stopped pulling on them.

An astronaut floats on board a space shuttle. He is weightless because he is falling around the world at the same speed as the shuttle itself.

Falling around the world

When a spacecraft is in orbit, it is moving around the world in a circle. An orbiting spacecraft or satellite is really falling around the Earth, but it is so far from the Earth that it keeps falling around the planet many thousands of times before it falls back down to the ground. The objects inside the spacecraft are moving at the same speed and so they float; they are weightless.

Small rocket engines are used to move to another orbit. To move farther away from the Earth, rockets are fired backwards for just the right amount of time. To move nearer the Earth, the rockets must be fired in front of the spacecraft. The engines must be on for just the right amount of time. If the rockets are on for too long or not long enough, the spacecraft will not move to the right orbit.

On the ground

Objects that are orbiting the world are tracked from stations on the ground using very large radars. These radars are located at different points around the world. They send out beams of radio waves, and the orbiting craft reflects some of them. The radar then picks up these reflections and can work out where the object is and where it is going.

When a spacecraft returns to Earth, it gets very hot as it comes back into the atmosphere. This is caused by gases rubbing against the spacecraft as it travels very fast. (Car tyres rubbing against the road get hot for the same reason.) Spacecraft that are designed to land have a thick heat shield, which stops the craft burning up on re-entry.

Astronauts sit in a dinghy after leaving the command module of their Moon rocket. The module, the only part of the rocket to return to Earth, landed in the sea using a parachute.

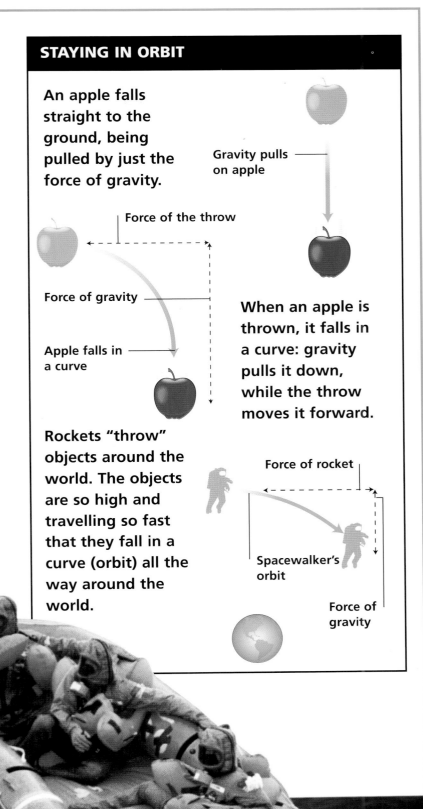

STAYING IN ORBIT

An apple falls straight to the ground, being pulled by just the force of gravity.

Gravity pulls on apple

Force of the throw

Force of gravity

Apple falls in a curve

When an apple is thrown, it falls in a curve: gravity pulls it down, while the throw moves it forward.

Rockets "throw" objects around the world. The objects are so high and travelling so fast that they fall in a curve (orbit) all the way around the world.

Force of rocket

Spacewalker's orbit

Force of gravity

The space shuttle

The space shuttle is the only spacecraft in use today that can fly into space, return to Earth safely and then fly back into space again. It is used to carry astronauts, satellites, and scientific equipment into space and bring back old or broken spacecraft to Earth.

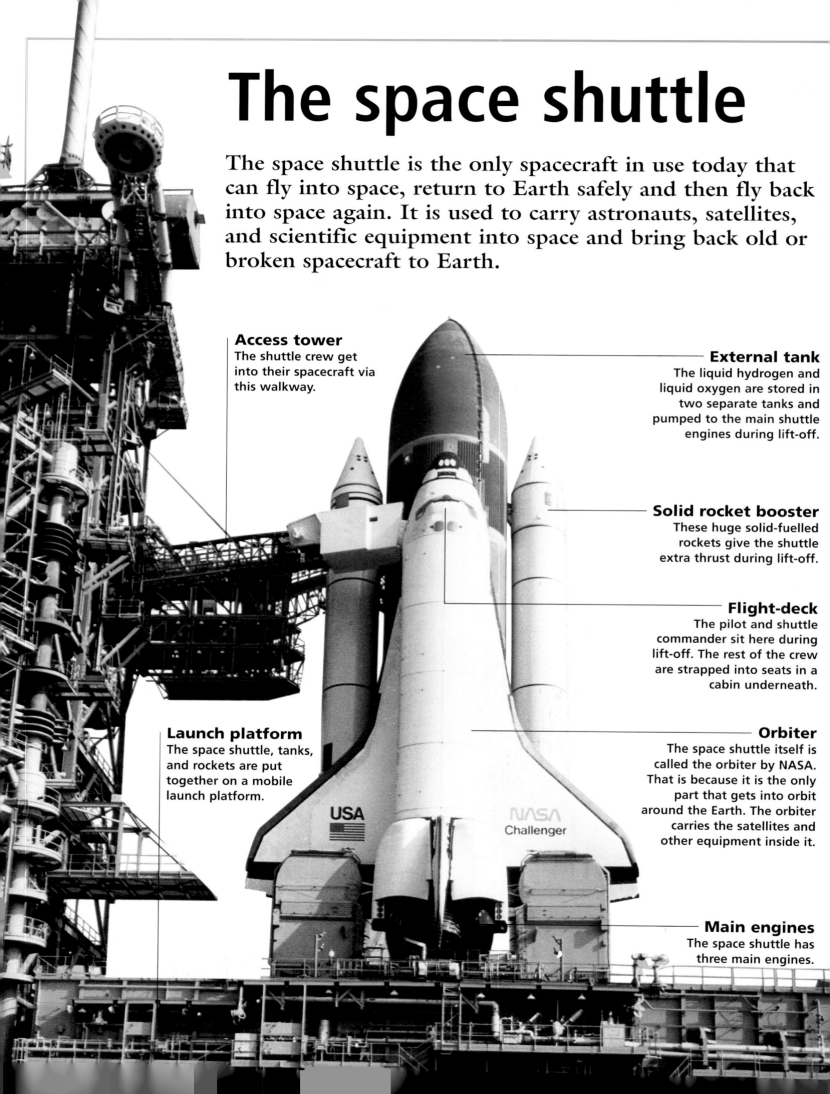

Access tower
The shuttle crew get into their spacecraft via this walkway.

External tank
The liquid hydrogen and liquid oxygen are stored in two separate tanks and pumped to the main shuttle engines during lift-off.

Solid rocket booster
These huge solid-fuelled rockets give the shuttle extra thrust during lift-off.

Flight-deck
The pilot and shuttle commander sit here during lift-off. The rest of the crew are strapped into seats in a cabin underneath.

Launch platform
The space shuttle, tanks, and rockets are put together on a mobile launch platform.

Orbiter
The space shuttle itself is called the orbiter by NASA. That is because it is the only part that gets into orbit around the Earth. The orbiter carries the satellites and other equipment inside it.

Main engines
The space shuttle has three main engines.

The launch and land sequence of the space shuttle makes it a very useful spacecraft for ferrying things into space. The shuttle can take off from Kennedy Space Center, Florida, and Vandenberg Air Force Base in California. The shuttle usually lands at its launch site, but in an emergency it can land at several runways around the world.

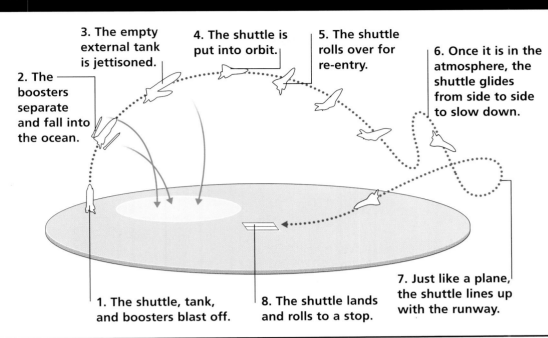

2. The boosters separate and fall into the ocean.

3. The empty external tank is jettisoned.

4. The shuttle is put into orbit.

5. The shuttle rolls over for re-entry.

6. Once it is in the atmosphere, the shuttle glides from side to side to slow down.

1. The shuttle, tank, and boosters blast off.

8. The shuttle lands and rolls to a stop.

7. Just like a plane, the shuttle lines up with the runway.

The shuttle orbiter is about the size of a 737 jet airliner (122 ft; 37m), and it can carry about 29 tons (28 tonnes) into space. (The Saturn V rockets lifted 50 tons [49 tonnes] but were destroyed in the process.)

The space shuttle has a two-stage launch. The huge solid rocket boosters (SRBs) provide most of the thrust to start with. After about two minutes the SRBs run out of fuel, and they fall away from the shuttle and into the ocean. The empty SRBs are collected from the water and reused.

The second stage of the shuttle launch comes from the shuttle engines. These three liquid-fuelled engines are on during lift-off, but become the only source of thrust after the SRBs fall away. Liquid hydrogen and oxygen are used as fuel and are stored in the huge external tank. Before the shuttle reaches its orbit, this empty tank also falls away. It breaks up and falls into the ocean.

The shuttle crew then use the small steering system rockets to position the shuttle in the right orbit. The shuttle orbits between 115 and 250 miles (184 and 400km) above the surface and travels at about 17,000 mph

The shuttle touches down at a speed of 220 mph (352km/h). Its landing wheels have brakes, and a parachute is used to slow the shuttle down.

(27,200km/h). Once in orbit, the crew launch satellites and perform experiments in the weightless conditions.

The shuttle re-enters the atmosphere flying backwards, with its smaller rockets firing to slow it down. Once the shuttle is gliding through the air, its wings start to work like a normal plane's, and the pilot steers into land. A shuttle's runway is 15,000 ft (4.5km) long.

Rockets to the rescue

Rockets are not just used for space travel and fireworks. Very fast military jet aircraft have rocket-powered ejector seats to help the pilot escape from a crashing plane.

Before fighter planes used jet engines, pilots could jump out of their planes when they were about to crash. But modern jet fighters fly so fast that it is impossible for pilots to do this. Instead, when an aircraft is in trouble, the pilot and crew can eject from the cockpit using rockets under their seats.

Flying by seat

Ejector seats use small solid-fuelled rockets. When the pilot decides it is time to leave the cockpit in a hurry, he or she pulls a handle, usually positioned above the pilot's head. The rockets are ignited, and the whole seat, including the pilot, shoots out the top of the plane in less than a second.

Because the plane is flying so fast, everything happens automatically after the pilot pulls the handle. A pilot could be injured by smashing through the plastic canopy that covers the top of the cockpit. So when the eject handle is pulled, the canopy is blown off by a small strip of explosives. Often the pilot pulls the handle over his or her head and this covers the face with a blast-proof blanket, which protects the pilot from the

A pilot ejects from a plane using the force of solid-fuelled rockets. The canopy shatters around him as he leaves the plane.

FACT FILE

○ Some ejector seats are designed to fly upward. So if the pilot ejects when the plane is flying on its side, the seat turns upward. This system makes sure that the pilot gets high enough for his or her parachute to work.

○ Ejector seats make flying safer for pilots but on a few occasions people on the ground have been killed by the seat falling on them.

○ The greatest height from which a pilot has jumped out of an aircraft is 102,000 ft (31,000m). That is nearly 20 miles (31km) high.

Pilots who have ejected from their crashing planes fall back to Earth on a parachute. The parachute opens automatically at the correct height.

canopy explosion. Usually these jet planes fly very high, where the air is too thin to breathe. The crew get their air from tanks on board the plane. When they eject, the crew's air supply is automatically changed to a bottle inside their ejector seats.

Out in the open

The rockets under the seat launch the pilot to a safe height above the crashing aircraft. The rockets only have enough fuel to fire for a few seconds and then the seat begins to fall back to the ground. Sensors in the seat check how high above the ground it is. When the seat falls to the right height, the pilot's parachute is automatically opened. The parachute slows the pilot and pulls him or her out of the seat. It is important that all this happens automatically because it is quite likely that the pilot will be unconscious because of the force of the ejection. Once the parachute has opened, the pilot can fall to the ground safely.

Since their invention about 50 years ago, ejector seats have saved about 7,000 pilots. They can save the lives of the crew members of planes that are flying upside down or travelling several miles above the ground.

Ejector seats also work in planes that are on the ground and even underwater.

Survival cabin

When the crew of an F-111 ejects, the entire crew cabin is forced away from the plane by rockets. Parachutes lower the cabin safely to the surface. If the cabin lands on water, it floats as a life raft. On land it can be used as a survival shelter. Huge parachutes are needed to slow down the falling capsule, or the force of the landing would kill the people inside.

Other rocket vehicles

As well as letting spacecraft fly into space, rocket engines have also been used to power very fast planes and make some ground vehicles move very quickly.

When jet planes were still being developed, rocket planes were flying at hundreds of miles an hour. The first rocket plane was called the Komet and was a fast fighter plane used by the Germans in World War II (1939–1945). These planes were very difficult to fly.

Another rocket-powered plane was the X-1. In 1947, flying in the X-1, U.S. pilot Chuck Yeager became the first person to travel faster than the speed of sound (650 mph; 1,040km/h).

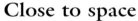

Close to space

A few years later, another rocket-powered plane, called the X-15, reached a speed of 4,250 mph (6,800km/h), which is nearly seven times the speed of sound. In this plane several pilots flew so high that they got to the edge of space. In fact, the X-15 flew to a height of 67 miles (107km). (The space shuttle orbits at a height of about 175 miles; 280km.) Because they flew so high, these pilots were called astronauts (from the Greek for *star* and *sailor*) like the people who fly into space today. People launched into orbit by the Russian space programme are called cosmonauts (*universe sailors*).

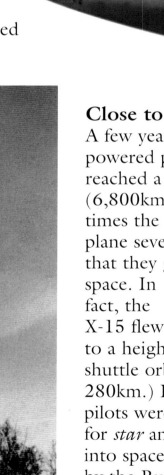

This experimental rocket-pack from 1967 was called the Bell Pogo. It used small rockets to lift one or two people into the air.

The X-1 rocket plane flown by Chuck Yeager, who was the first person to travel faster than the speed of sound in 1947.

Rocket boost

Rockets are still used in some planes. Military planes that are too large and heavy to take off from short runways sometimes have liquid-fuelled rockets strapped to them. The rockets help the planes speed up to take-off speed more quickly than they would with just their jet engines.

The same idea has been used for cars. Many people have built cars powered by rocket engines, hoping that they will travel faster than any other car. However, the world's fastest car, which can travel faster than the speed of sound, is powered by two jet engines. Rocket cars run out of fuel very quickly and that makes them very hard to drive safely. This is because they start off very heavy and soon become light as the fuel is used up. Changing weight like this makes the car likely to flip over or swerve around when travelling at high speeds.

ROCKET CAR

You will need a rectangular piece of cardboard, four polystyrene cups, four pins, a flexible straw, tape and a balloon.

1 Cut the bottom off the cups, and pin them to the cardboard to make wheels. Make sure they spin easily. Tape the end of the balloon over the end of the short part of the straw and tape the long part of the straw to the cardboard.

2 Blow up the balloon, and squeeze the end of the straw to keep the air in. Place the car on a smooth surface and let it go!

Fun and danger

Firework rockets have been used for many years as forms of entertainment, to alert rescuers to the position of sinking ships, and for signalling across large distances.

F ireworks are small rockets powered by solid fuel. Gunpowder is the main fuel used, and other chemicals are added to the fuel to make the firework's explosion very bright and colourful.

What is in a firework?

Gunpowder is a mixture of sulphur, a yellow chemical; charcoal, a fuel made by heating wood; and saltpetre, a white, chalky chemical found on rocks and in soil. Firecrackers are the simplest fireworks. They are just a tube of gunpowder with a fuse. When the fuse sets fire to the gunpowder, the gunpowder explodes with a loud bang.

Another type of firework is a sparkler. Sparklers are long fireworks that do not go "bang" but burn slowly from one end to the other. The colour of the sparkler depends on the chemicals in them.

Most fireworks are a mixture of these two types. The gunpowder rocket fuel launches them into the sky and causes them to explode. Little cubes of coloured chemicals are set on fire by the gunpowder explosion and this gives the firework its impressive colours.

Not just for fun

Flares are rockets that are very similar to fireworks. But instead of being for fun, flares are used in an emergency. For example, if a

Firework rockets are just like other solid-fuelled rockets. However, they are not toys and can cause very serious burns if they are not used properly.

FACT FILE

○ Firework fuels were probably first used as signals and alarm devices. They were not used for entertainment until rocket technology was developed for military uses.

○ Gunpowder, as the name suggests, was also the explosive used in the first guns.

○ Coloured fireworks were not common until the 19th century, after scientists had discovered how to mix the right chemicals.

plane has crashed in a remote area or a ship has sunk at sea, the survivors can fire flares to attract the attention of people coming to rescue them. Flares are fired from a pistol but work like firework rockets. They are usually orange, so they can be easily seen during the day and at night.

Rockets are used in another way to help rescue people. Lifeboats use small firework-like rockets to carry ropes from their boat to the deck of a sinking ship. The rescuers fire the rocket over the ship and the ropes fall onto the deck. The crew can then use the ropes to climb to safety.

Flares are fired from pistols such as these. Pulling the trigger ignites the fuel and launches the flare.

Above: Firework displays have impressed people for a thousand years. Many holidays and special events are celebrated with huge public displays.

An illustration of the X-33 Venture Star, which may one day replace the space shuttle.

Flying into the future

Rocket engines are still the best way of launching spacecraft. New types of spacecraft are being designed that will be cheaper and easier to use than rockets and space shuttles.

The first space shuttle flew in 1981, and it is still the only type of reusable spacecraft being used. However, NASA will soon be using a new spacecraft to carry astronauts, parts of space stations, and satellites into space and return safely to Earth.

The Venture Star, or the X-33, as it is also called, will not need booster rockets or several stages to get into orbit because it will use

very efficient rocket engines. The X-33 will be launched from a ramp and then re-enter the atmosphere in the same way as a space shuttle and glide back to Earth and land like an aeroplane. The special shape of the X-33 allows it to glide and also carry enough fuel to get into space.

The X-33's engines are called linear aerospike rockets. They use the same sort of liquid fuel as normal rocket engines, but they do not have nozzles. Therefore the hot exhaust gases are released along the whole width of the rear of the spacecraft.

Aerospike engines provide more thrust than other rockets because they are more efficient and cause less drag (air resistance). Unlike most normal rocket engines, they can also be used to steer the spacecraft.

New ways to travel

If the X-33 is a success, then people will be able to travel into space more cheaply than ever before, making it easier for them to build places to live and work there. Rocket-powered space planes could carry passengers to cities around the world in just minutes rather than many hours.

Rocket lifeboat

Another new type of spacecraft is being built to let the astronauts working on the International Space Station escape in an emergency and return safely to Earth. The X-38 has small rocket engines for steering in space. Like the X-33, it glides down toward the ground, only this spacecraft has a huge parachute to help it land safely.

Above: The huge parachute of an X-38 spacecraft being tested. The X-38 cannot fly into space on its own but it can bring astronauts back to Earth.

Below: An artist's impression of a space plane that will carry cargo and people from place to place around the world in just a few hours instead of days and weeks.

Glossary

AFT—a word originally used by sailors meaning toward the rear of the ship.

COOLANT—a liquid that is used to keep rocket fuel cold so that it stays liquid.

DRAG—a force that acts on objects that are moving through air or water, slowing them down. Also called air or water resistance.

ELEVON—a flap on the wing of the space shuttle used to steer the spacecraft when it is gliding through the atmosphere.

EQUATOR—the imaginary line that runs around the middle of the globe, marking the point halfway between the poles.

EXHAUST GAS—the gas produced by burning rocket fuel. Exhaust gases force the rocket into the air.

FORCE—a push or pull on an object that makes it speed up or slow down.

FUEL INJECTOR—the device that sprays the rocket fuel into the combustion chamber.

In the future a small rocket may be launched from a high-flying larger rocket or aeroplane.

GLIDE—to fly without using any power from the engines.

HEAT SHIELD—a part of a spacecraft that is designed to protect against the high temperatures caused by re-entry.

KEROSENE—A type of fuel made from petroleum oil and used as rocket fuel and in jet engines.

LINEAR AEROSPIKE—a type of rocket engine that does not have a circular nozzle but fires out the exhaust gases through a gap along the width of the spacecraft.

OXIDIZER—one of the liquids used for rocket fuel. The oxidizer, usually liquid oxygen, makes the other fuel liquid burn when they are mixed together.

PAYLOAD—a rocket's cargo, such as satellites, scientists, or space stations; the load that pays for the rocket to launch.

PROPELLANT—a liquid, such as liquid hydrogen, in a rocket fuel that burns rapidly when it is mixed with the oxidizer.

RE-ENTRY—when a spacecraft travels back into the Earth's atmosphere. Air resistance causes the spacecraft to get very hot.

SATELLITE—an object that orbits a planet or star. The Moon is the Earth's largest natural satellite. Artificial satellites are launched into space by rockets.

WEIGHTLESS—how people feel when they and everything around them are falling at the same speed.

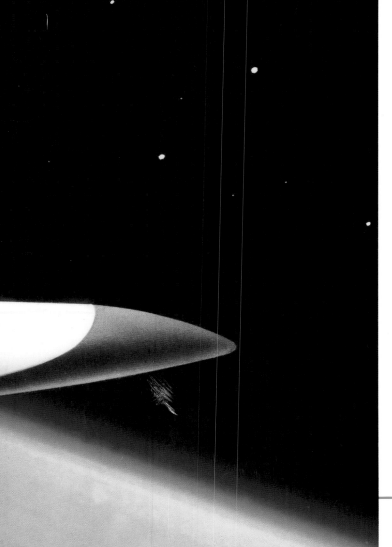

FURTHER INFORMATION

Books to read:
Blasting Off by Steve Otfinoski. Benchmark Books; New York, NY, 1999.
The History of Rockets by Ron Miller. Franklin Watts; New York, NY, 1999.

Web sites to look at:
http://www.spaceflight.nasa.gov
http://www.venturestar.com
http://www.thiokol.com
http://www.boeing.com
http://www.jsc.nasa.gov/pao/students

Index

PICTURE CREDITS BBL 3t, 26r **Corbis** 8tr Michael Freeman, 23tr George Hall, 27bl Michael Freeman, 27r Judy Griesedieck **Mary Evans Picture Library** 4t **Genesis Space Photo Library** 9t and cover, 10bl, 13c, 15l, 15tr, 18t and cover, 24bl, 30 & 31b **Robert Hunt Library** 5br **NASA** 21cr, 28t, 29tr, **TRH Pictures** 3b, 5tl, 14t, 16c, 19b, 20b and cover, 22l, 24 & 25t, 29b (t-top b-bottom r-right l-left c-center)